believe

A Mother's Memoir of Loss,
Hope and Trusting Again

FUNKE OHAM

Believe — A Mother's Memoir of Loss, Hope and Trusting Again
Copyright © 2023 by Funke Oham

Published by BUTTERFLY PUBLISHING

All rights reserved. No part of this book may be reproduced or transmitted, in any form, or by any means without the prior permission of both the copyright owner and the above publisher of this book.

The scripture versions cited in this book are identified in my hope affirmations, which hereby become a part of this copyright page.

ISBN: 979-8-8631980-6-4

Printed in the United Kingdom

DEDICATION

This book is dedicated to my super amazing husband, Charles, my heavenly babies Isaac and Faith and both my sons.

I am grateful to my parents, family, church, mentors, medical professionals, friends and colleagues who supported me on my journey to motherhood.

To all the women who have walked this path and are still walking this path, thank you for allowing me to be a part of your journey and to be your compassionate friend.

ACKNOWLEDGMENTS

I am standing here, only because God was there for me when my world turned upside down. He indeed brought His word to pass to give me a hope, a future and bring me to an expected end. Thank you Lord, for being in my story even when I doubted and was filled with fear. I look back over the last twenty years and all I have to say is thank you, Jesus.

A special thanks to my editor, Peggy Bartlett, for understanding my heart and retaining my voice. I will cherish your kind words too. I am so grateful our paths crossed.

Michelle VanGeest, thank you for your excellent type setting service. Hence the reason I keep coming back to you. I am especially grateful for your patience on this particular book project. You accommodated all my ideas and changes. Thanks for bringing to life my manuscript and providing a great reading experience.

TABLE OF CONTENTS

Foreword ... 9

Introduction ... 11

Chapter 1   Butterflies ... 15

Chapter 2   Finally Pregnant ... 23

Chapter 3   11:12 a.m. ... 37

Chapter 4   Valentine's Eve ... 53

Chapter 5   Christmas Eve ... 71

Chapter 6   Paradigm Shift ... 91

Chapter 7   Promises ... 113

Only If ... 132

About the Author ... 134

FOREWORD

I read the book *Believe* from cover to cover in a couple of hours. I simply couldn't put it down!

The book is a gripping detailed yet concise account of Funke's journey as a newlywed bride through the joy of getting pregnant twice in quick succession and the devastation of then losing the children prematurely.

It is an honest and sincere no holds barred account leaving you feeling every pain she felt, hoping against hope for her when the crushing disappointments came and literally dancing for joy with her when her time of rejoicing came with the live birth of a healthy baby the third time round!

Funke describes how she was so disappointed in God and wondered how He could say He loved her and yet let her go through such pain. She takes us on her redemption journey as she works herself back by prayer and study of God's word to a place of faith and trust in Him again.

This book will be a blessing to anyone who has lost a baby or a loved one as Funke holds your hand and helps you sift through the confusion, anger and hurt till you get to that place where you can laugh again, love again and trust again.

Believe

You come away understanding that God's love for you transcends any pain or hurt you may feel and know that with faith in Him, joy always comes in the morning.

I commend the author for this beautifully written, practical and easy-to-read guide through times of trouble and congratulate her and her most supportive husband Charles on the testimony of happy parenting that they can now share.

Yewande Zaccheaus
Author, *God's Waiting Room* Books 1-4
Executive Producer, The Wait

INTRODUCTION

After getting married in my mid-twenties, my life was all mapped out, and my expectation then was that everything would go according to plan. This included completing postgraduate studies, passing my driving test, starting a family, and living happily ever after. Of course, life presents us with challenges but what lay ahead of me came as a total bolt from the blue. From the young age of 10, I was aware that some women had difficulties with conception and women lost young children. However, I did not understand the impact of such calamities in the lives of the families involved until conception eluded me for sixteen months and losing our first son due to a stillbirth despite being a full-term pregnancy.

The ensuing months brought the guilt phase, self-blame, and the why me syndrome that epitomizes the bereaved. After much reflection, counsel, and prayer, my only consolation was the confidence that the cause(s) of such misfortune would never occur again. Lo, and behold, our daughter was born prematurely nine months later at 23 weeks. Although she was born quite early, we were quite confident she would survive and reach full term, and we would take her home. After all, this is the 21st century, and the care of premature

Believe

babies has come a long way. Alas, she slipped away after a ten-hour battle.

In as much as many friends, acquaintances and family were supportive, a few unintentionally caused more pain with their attitude and comments. While going through this "why me" period, I came across many women in similar positions who were equally perplexed. My search for answers day in and day out yielded no answers from the medical profession, websites, blogs, family, or friends. As a practicing Christian who loves God, I could not comprehend why He allowed me to lose two babies in succession and why we were chosen out of the millions of people on earth to go through such unbearable pain.

If God let me down twice, could He be trusted to rescue me?

Without a shadow of a doubt, I now completely believe God loves me. His promise to make me a mum would be a reality, and God was not the source of my misfortune. The prospect of having more children was something to be thankful for. However, I still had to work through the maze of disappointment, aloneness, confusion, and only ifs until a sermon changed my thinking one day.

Countless women and families have been through a similar situation, or perhaps you have been through a different situation that has brought much pain. This

Introduction

book aims to share my experience and help you move from that painful situation to a point where you can be free, hope, and try again even though you cannot turn back the hand of time.

Butterflies

1

MARCH 29, 2003

"This is it," I thought as I sat in the back seat of the Mercedes Benz being driven from Stratford to Oval on our way to my wedding. No amendments could be made now. Whatever preparation (for the day and as a single lady) that remained undone remained so. I thought to myself, had I made the right choice? I was quite certain I had. But it was too late for that. I decided to relax and enjoy the last conversation (nothing major) I would have with my dad bearing my maiden name.

I could not help wondering if my day would go beautifully well with no unpleasant surprises. I chose to leave my phone with my brother to prevent me from making and receiving calls and avoid being stressed out (trying to curb my perfectionist tendency). It is wonderful to

Butterflies

have a team of capable friends you can always count on.

I actually arrived at the church a few minutes before 11:00 a.m. I didn't want to keep my prince charming waiting. Like most other girls, you have fantasies about your wedding day as a little girl. As we waited in the car, I had to pinch myself. It was me who was getting married. My husband and I would be the center of attention—not that I like much of it. I felt honored, loved, and appreciated to have our friends and family share such a blissful occasion with us.

One of the ushers, a friend, gestured that it was okay for me to alight from the car and enter the church. Just not yet, as I had a full bladder, and I would not want to dash into the ladies during our vows lest people think I was doing a runner like Julia Roberts in Runaway Bride.

It was hilarious having to use the toilet in my wedding dress. I didn't want to get it dirty as it was an ivory dress with a long train. I managed somehow. In hindsight, it makes much sense to keep wedding dresses simple. Most wedding dress designers probably do not consider the practicalities of wearing some dresses and going to the toilet. By the end of the day, the bottom of my dress was quite dirty as it had swept the floor all day.

The church ceremony went well. There were also a few tears of joy—thanks, Liz. You initiated that! The exhortation focused on the storms of life; in the midst of

Believe

the storm, we can rest because Jesus would be in the boat with us and bring peace. Thank God I listened but maybe not totally, as my mind was on so many things, because this word was one of the anchors that kept me going when the unexpected occurred some years later.

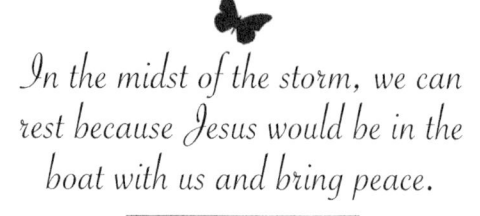

> *In the midst of the storm, we can rest because Jesus would be in the boat with us and bring peace.*

The reception was grand and full of butterflies. Not in the flesh but in theme. Why butterflies? To remind me of the swarms of butterflies in my tummy while courting. Nothing happened in case your mind has gone places. As a dear friend of mine usually says, "I am holy and innocent." After the reception, we headed for Marriot Hotel in Waltham Abbey, where we were supposed to stay for two nights and then fly out to Fuerteventura in Spain.

On getting to the hotel, we expected our check-in to be straightforward, but it was not. The bank had canceled my husband's card because a number of purchases had been paid for in the last couple of days.

What upset us was that they did not attempt to contact my husband regarding the recent transactions. If they did, they would have found out our wedding was around the corner hence the recent expenses. Whoever came up with the idea of not putting all your eggs in your basket must have foreseen what would happen. Thank God my husband had some cash to pay the hotel bill; otherwise, we would have spent our first night at home.

What lay ahead of me and us? What will our future hold? As the saying goes, if you fail to plan, you plan to fail. So, like most people, we had plans, and I did have a few of my own.

BABY TIME

A few months before our wedding, I started a Post Graduate Certificate in Education (PGCE), intending to finish the course in eighteen months, have a baby, and teach for two years (prerequisite) for doing a Master's in Educational Psychology and then become an Educational Psychologist. If only life was that simple.

I did finish the course but discovered towards the end that teaching was not for me, and I would not be able to balance this career with my other charitable commitments. That was a big blow, especially as the last term was the hardest and the most challenging

Believe

time of my career. Each time I went past the primary school, which was close to my home, where I did my teaching practice, I felt very sad. I wanted to avoid the place totally, and it brought bad memories. I had to deal with my disappointment, let go of the Educational Psychology career, and choose to do something else I am very interested in. I am glad to say that feeling has lifted, and it matters no more. I was excited that it would still lead to my ultimate career goal.

Going back to the drawing board, the plan was to try for a baby once completing the course, as I did not want to have a baby while studying for the PGCE. I felt I couldn't cope and wanted to spend quality time with our baby without the pressure of studies. With some support from my husband, I decided to go on the pill against my mum's advice. Naughty girl.

Of course, I was aware it could take some time for conception to occur once I came off the pill, but I was hoping it would not take long. A friend of mine was lucky as she fell pregnant immediately after she came off the pill; I hoped it would be a similar case for me.

I came off the pill just as I completed the course and believed I'd conceive in at most three to four months. At first, I was not worried as I thought it was early days. However, by month four, I began to think, "What is going on?" As a firm believer in faith, I refused to be discouraged, and I was aware it could take up to a year to become pregnant after coming off the pill, but I was not mentally prepared to wait a year.

As the months went by, I saw my period month after month, which was so upsetting, and I thought to myself each month, please, not again. One month my period was very late. We were quite sure I was pregnant and nearly went out to buy the pregnancy kit, but I told my husband we should give it a few more days before checking. Alas, a day or two after this, my period showed up. Needless to say, this news was so discouraging.

It got to a point we just had to keep going as we all know nothing happens if we do not try. Every new month brought some dread with it. What if I was not pregnant? However, it also brought us another opportunity. It very well could be this new month I became pregnant.

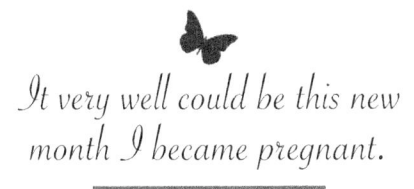

It very well could be this new month I became pregnant.

After a year, we were still anticipating conception. I never expected to be faced with such a challenge in my life. I had followed the advice of the nurse I saw some months back, eating well and resting. Was something wrong with one or both of us? I did not want to entertain this line of thought. We thought we should go to the

Believe

doctor and say we had been trying for one year without success. Going there would make me so vulnerable, and I did not want to be in that position. We decided to give it a few more months. If nothing still happened, we would consider seeking counsel.

Two months after we were still at it, it was now August 2005. My period was late this month. Due to prior experience, I did not want to get my hopes high just in case my period was late again and nothing had happened.

Around this time, we went for a christening, and I was so unhappy and moody the whole day. I couldn't place my finger on what was making me feel this way, which was an unusual feeling. Over the next few days, I still felt the same way. Shortly after we came home on one of those nights, my husband and I sat on the stairs outside our front door and talked. It then dawned on my husband that I might be pregnant. Perhaps that explained the moodiness?

Finally Pregnant

2

NO KEBABS, PLEASE

Was I or wasn't I pregnant? I could not wait to find out. It was the first of September 2006. We decided to go to Waltham Abbey (where we spent our wedding night). We strolled along the high street, not that there was much to see. As it was early afternoon, my husband and I had lunch in one of the cafes.

Then it was time to get the kit. Being the shy person I am — which some people will find hard to believe — I did not feel comfortable purchasing the pregnancy kit. I tried talking my husband into it. He gently coaxed me into going for it. I lingered around the display unit for a while, trying to muster the courage to pick up the kit.

Eventually, I did.

Finally Pregnant

Are you wondering why I lingered? Well, I look much younger than my age. I don't like people having the impression that I am a teenager who may be pregnant and strangers asking me questions or wondering if I may be pregnant.

I walked up to the counter, made no eye contact with the lady serving at the counter, and made sure my wedding ring was visible when I was paying for the kit. I — actually we — couldn't wait to get home. This was the moment we have awaited anxiously, expectantly, and prayerfully for the last sixteen months.

> *This was the moment we have awaited anxiously, expectantly, and prayerfully for the last sixteen months.*

When we got home, a friend of my husband's was waiting for us. He came over to assist him with his car. I waited for some time, but curiosity got the better of me. I called out to my husband and told him I wanted to go ahead and find out. I thought he was not keen on the procedure but on the result. I went ahead, got the urine specimen, and Charles walked into the

Believe

bathroom when I was about to insert the stick in the urine. We both took a pause, and in it went. The next few seconds seemed like an eternity. At first, no line appeared, and I thought not this time. But on closer inspection, the test was positive. I was in shock. I just stared at the stick, did not let go, and exclaimed, "I am PREGNANT!"

What a joyous discovery. When you get such news, you probably want to tell the world. Well, not if you are me. Being the cautious type or rather predisposed to a secretive trait, I didn't want a soul to know, at least not yet. How did I manage to convince my husband to go along with me? It must be love! I'm joking, but actually, it is. As this was my very first pregnancy, I thought it was better to wait for the end of the first trimester (first three months), which is the most critical stage in pregnancy, and hopefully, if I came through this hurdle, there was nothing to worry about again. How naïve!

FIRST TRIMESTER

Those three months were long and hard, especially with family and colleagues. As the usual practice was, each time I spoke to my parents, they reiterated they were praying for us and waited patiently for a hint of such news. As it was my custom, I reassured them to keep on trusting God and avoid worrying. I had to be extra cautious at work not to let the cat out of the bag, especially when the smell of certain foods, unexpectedly consumed by others, was off-putting.

I finally reached the twelve weeks mark. It seemed like ages before I arrived at this milestone. You may be wondering if I suffered from morning sickness. Guess I was lucky. I escaped the feeling. However, the sight of Kebab shops, which are numerous on the bus journey home from Walthamstow to Chingford, made me feel sick. The way around that was to keep my eyes shut till I got home (I tried). Even with my eyes shut, my mind sometimes managed to conjure up the image of the Kebab shop, and hey, I had to deal with suppressing the sick feeling. Writing about this now makes me feel sick.

We were looking forward to our first ultrasound. What would our baby look like? Would it be an emotional time for us? Will there be any abnormalities? Hopefully, not. Other couples were also at the ultrasound section. Not everyone there was first-time parents or first trimesters. There was a little bit of chit-chat with other mums and dads. As time passed, I just wanted the sonographer to hurry up and call us in. The lady sonographer was relatively young and didn't seem too friendly, but she was professional.

Believe

The gel applied to my tummy was cold but tolerable. After locating the baby, she took some measurements before turning the screen towards us. She pointed out the different parts of our baby's body, and everything seemed okay — what a joy and relief. This experience made the pregnancy seem more real after seeing our baby on ultrasound. She pointed out that there were two small cysts in my womb. When I asked her about it, she didn't say much and mumbled that the midwife or doctor would talk me through it.

Of course, we paid and took home a copy of our baby's scan. From three months, we could tell that the back of the baby's head was protruding, which runs in my family and is commonly referred to as ogo. The scan was a treasured possession, and whenever I needed reassurance that our baby was real or I felt physically exhausted, I got it out and dreamed of my future as a mum. That brought on huge smiles and made the discomfort a small price to pay.

After this, we decided to tell my parents to put their minds at rest. They were over the moon. Then went my mum's list of dos and don'ts, and every conversation from that day forward was, you know what; rest, eat well, and do not lift heavy things. We also informed my husband's family, and they were all excited.

DOLL OR CAR?

On my way home from work one day, I overheard some girls talking about their friend who had a miscarriage at four months. This made me a bit concerned that the first trimester is not the end of mishaps. But I tried to focus on having a good outcome with the pregnancy and believed everything would go well. It was liberating when I got to the four-month mark.

The twenty-week scan was another major milestone and an exciting day for us. By this time, our baby would be much bigger, and of course, we could stop calling the baby, baby and refer to them as he or she if we found out the baby's sex. Everything was fine on the ultrasound.

When we were asked if we wanted to know the sex of the baby, I said no, and my husband said yes. Although we had previously discussed, we wouldn't find out to keep it a surprise. My husband's justification for knowing was to let us know what clothes to buy for the baby. We had a strong inclination that it would be a boy even before I became pregnant.

Charles being the keen observer that he is, before the sonographer said it was a boy, picked it up from the screen (we agreed that he should tell us our baby's sex). We both blurted out, "It's a boy!" just as he was about to tell us, as we always knew we would have a boy

Believe

first. I am still unsure how Charles figured that out, as I cannot tell when I look at the screen I just cannot tell.

I refused to tell a soul the sex of our baby as I felt it would spoil the fun of keeping people guessing. Plus, it is wonderful to find out whether the baby is a boy or a girl upon his or her arrival. As the norm is once a baby is born, people want to know what you had, then the baby's weight, and of course, whether it was a normal or assisted delivery.

So far, so good. I felt strong and healthy. I actually started getting used to eating my five portions of fruit and vegetables. My manager found me interesting to watch as I arrayed my portions of fruit and vegetables on my desk first thing in the morning and my goal was to ensure I ate it all up before I left work. I am glad to say I did. However, it was a struggle at times.

By the time I got to thirty-two weeks, I was anxious to leave work and be at home. Being the hardworking, over-committed person I am, that was a long way coming.

WHAT'S IN A NAME?

I did not know that choosing a name for our baby would be such a difficult task. It is probably to do with wanting that perfect name that truly embodies who your child is and would be. When people asked, "Have you chosen a name yet?" we would say no. They were surprised that we had not by this stage. But I always said that by the time baby arrives, there will be a name for him or her. As they did not know the baby's sex, there were suggestions for boys' and girls' names. But none were quite right.

My husband and I had our own brainstorming name session, but we still had not come up with a name. On one particular day, I remember he visited a friend and returned excited. He had a name. In the middle of his conversation with his friend, his friend also talked about someone else with that name, and he felt it was a confirmation. I thought it seemed his mind was made up, and I hoped I would like the name too.

We finally decided on the name Isaac for our son. Why Isaac? I believe that to my husband, Isaac would accomplish great things and carry on from where he stopped. However, for me, Isaac was a child of promise and laughter.

FALSE ALARM

I woke up one morning and found my bed wet. The first thought that came into my head was, did I wet my bed? That has not happened to me since I was a child—a sign of excellent potty training. Thanks, mum. What was it then? Then it dawned on me, did my water break? The thought brought trepidation as I was not ready for our baby. I still had one more week at work and had not done any baby shopping.

I was thirty-five weeks pregnant at this point. I had heard of women having their babies early. I quickly went through the pregnancy booklet I was given by my midwife. I was unsure if this was bedwetting or early labor, so we decided I should go to my doctor. I had an appointment with my doctor that day, and the locum doctor who attended to me advised me to go to the hospital immediately to be on the safe side. I made my way there immediately. I rang my husband, who later joined me.

I was kept for hours before a doctor attended to me. We are talking about the National Health Service (aka NHS). I was examined and informed that my waters had not broken, but I would be admitted so they could keep a close eye on me. I couldn't believe it. I hate hospitals. I had never slept overnight in a hospital apart from when I was born.

You would not believe it, but the following day was my birthday. After a long day, I was eventually discharged and told to come in every other day so the baby and I could be monitored. There was no reason to worry as it was just routine monitoring. I was too tired even to celebrate what was left of the day by the time I finally got home.

I was relieved when the following week ended, and I was a free woman in one sense, as I was not too far away with the arrival of our son. Apart from my paid job, I also ran a women's network. At this point, we had a new staff member, and I spent the remaining few weeks handing my duties over to her, even right up to my due date. Typical of me, but that kept me active a few days a week.

On my thirty-seventh week appointment, which fell on Easter Monday, I went in for a routine appointment with my midwife. On checking my blood pressure, she felt it was a bit raised and asked me to go to the assessment unit upstairs for a blood test. As usual, that took hours. At one point, one of the nurses said they might keep me in overnight, pending the test result. Deep down in my heart, I did not want to stay. Moreover, my cousin and his family were coming to visit us later that afternoon. While waiting stuck on the hospital bed, I realized I had too many loose ends to tie, and I had to prepare myself mentally for the arrival of our son and let others take care of any unfinished business.

I was glad when they finally said everything was okay and I could go home. One week came and went, and I went in the following week to see my midwife, who insisted she had to see me the following week at our last meeting. I missed my bus and had to take a different route to the health center. I eventually got there five minutes late. I hurried up the stairs, knocked on the door as the norm was to notify my midwife of my arrival, and sat in the waiting area. Five minutes later, I knocked again as she still had not responded, which was quite unusual. I thought she was with another patient. It then dawned on me that no one was inside the room. I went downstairs to the reception area and asked after my midwife. I was told she left some minutes ago. I was quite surprised she left without calling me to find out my whereabouts, especially as she insisted I see her that week, and I was only five minutes late.

I rang her at the hospital two to three times that week and left messages, but she did not return my calls. I found out later that she was away. By this time, my every other day visit to the hospital was one to two times a week. I went in for one final ultrasound on the 26th of April, as my consultant felt our baby was small for his gestation age when he saw me some months back. The sonographer informed my husband and me that everything was fine with our baby and that there was nothing to worry about.

My mum had arrived and was staying over to assist us with our newborn baby.

By this time, I could not wait for Isaac to arrive. Everything was nearly sorted, and I was ready to hold my bundle of joy and experience the wonder of motherhood. There were phone calls here and there to find out if our baby had arrived.

On the 30th of April, 2006, we went to church as usual. It was a beautiful day. After service, believe it or not, I went and did my last-minute food shopping. That was not all; a friend of my husband invited my husband to an event. So, after the shopping, we popped in there.

We got home, made dinner, then ate. Just before dinner, I felt a slight pain in my tummy that came on and off, but it was manageable. Charles had to pop out, and I watched a movie on TV with my mum while he was away. I cannot remember what it was, but we enjoyed it. After the movie, mum and I went up to bed. I lay down to sleep and had to get up to wee. I lay down again and felt the urge to revisit the toilet.

I was ready to hold my bundle of joy and experience the wonder of motherhood.

This happened over and over again. After a while, I had a runny stool (diarrhea). It then occurred to me that it may be early signs of labor. My mum called out to find out if I was okay. I told her I was. Then I went back to lie down. It was then that the pain intensified. I read through the pregnancy book I was given, confirming I was in the early stages of labor. I rang the hospital and was told to stay home until things progressed.

By this time, I couldn't even concentrate fully. My mum insisted we go to the hospital and ignore what I was told. We got my bags and headed for the hospital around 3:00 a.m. By this time, I found it hard to talk, sit or lie down in the car as I was in excruciating pain. The drive to the hospital was around twenty minutes. As soon as we walked through the door, the receptionist at the maternity department told us to go to the labor ward. My head was twirling around, I couldn't keep still, didn't know where to touch to soothe the pain (my tummy, back, or head), and all I could think of was this is how labor is meant to be.

11:12 a.m.

3

WHIPPS CROSS HOSPITAL

We buzzed the bell, and we were allowed into the labor ward. One of the midwives led us to a delivery room. I was given a hospital gown to change into and told to lie down on the bed. I could not even sit on the bed, let alone lie down. The midwife gently persuaded me to lie down for her to monitor our baby. After a couple of minutes, although in much agony, I managed to lie down on the bed. She then applied the gel and tried to find our baby's heartbeat. She tried a few times but eventually located it at the far side of my tummy. It was time to attach the strap to my tummy, and my baby's heartbeat began to be monitored.

During this time, my blood pressure was 163/102, which was very high for me compared to my booking BP

11:12 a.m.

of 90/60 at week ten of pregnancy. I was asked for a urine sample but could not provide one as I did not feel the urge to urinate. I basically lost track of time and was in and out of sleep as I was exhausted. I guess sleeping was a way to escape the continuous and unbearable pain. After a few hours, even the strap attached to my tummy was a source of discomfort and prevented me from massaging my tummy to alleviate the pain naturally. I asked the nurse to please remove it but still monitor our baby with a Doppler (handheld device). On removing it, she asked me if I would be able to give her some urine for checking. I went to the toilet and tried but had no luck.

I wanted to pass urine, but it felt like I had been sewn up and was prevented from doing so. In my mind, I actually thought, will I ever be able to pass urine normally, and perhaps something had gone wrong? At that moment, urinating was the least of my worries. I wanted the pain to go away and to deliver my baby.

One of the doctors popped in around 5:30 a.m. I recognized her from my frequent visit to the Assessment Unit for a review. I was encouraged to use some pain relief due to the amount of pain I was in and my increased blood pressure. I eventually agreed. I'm not sure if I was afraid the pain relief might hurt my baby or just wasn't keen on having any form of pain relief. To be honest, I cannot even remember my reason for

Believe

declining. The doctor instructed the midwife to take some blood to check for signs of preeclampsia, monitor my blood pressure closely, and carry out a urine dip. The Midwife took the blood and went away.

At around 7:00 a.m., another midwife woke me up from sleep. She introduced herself and told me she had taken over from her colleague and would like to monitor my baby. She applied the gel and tried to find the baby's heartbeat to guide her on where to place the disc to read and monitor his heartbeat. Like the other midwife, she didn't find the heartbeat immediately and kept on trying. At first, I was not concerned as it can sometimes take a while to locate a baby's heartbeat, especially when they are very active.

After many unsuccessful attempts, I became a bit panicky and asked her to please get someone else. She called another midwife, but still no success. Another more senior midwife was called in, but still nothing. As I was highly drowsy due to the pain relief injection I was given, I did not realize how much time (over one hour) was spent by these midwives going back and forth trying to locate my son's heartbeat.

My mum suggested they get our baby out earlier as she felt my labor was a bit long and due to the discomfort I was in. The most senior midwife present advised that because I was still in early labor, it was better to wait and let labor progress naturally.

11:12 a.m.

Apparently, they thought that because my bladder was distended, that prevented them from locating his heartbeat. I was asked to go to the toilet, but I still did nothing. Hence, I was told to lie back, and some tube (catheter) was inserted into me (very uncomfortable and wouldn't want to be in that position again) to enable the urine flow. The accumulated urine was drained, and I was examined.

Despite draining my urine, no heartbeat was found. It was only then that a registrar was called in. My mum was not in the room when all this was going on. I wondered where she was but was more focused on them finding my baby's heartbeat. The registrar examined my tummy and requested that scanning equipment be brought in. He checked, and then a consultant was called in who rechecked with an Ultrasonography and informed us that there was no heartbeat. I had a sudden placental abruption, and Isaac had no chance of survival. The abruption was linked to preeclampsia, which affects four million women worldwide every year and causes complications in two to three percent of UK pregnancies. This condition is the leading cause of death in mothers and babies (Tommy's website; baby charity).

Was I expecting this? Not in a million years, you bet, not that I would live to a million years on this side of eternity. I guess it was one of those times you think,

"Wake me up. This must be a bad dream." All I said was 'Jesus' when the consultant told us his finding. My mum entered the room and was devastated to hear the news. Apparently, she left the room to go into the car to pray.

It was one of those times you think, "Wake me up. This must be a bad dream."

I just nodded when the consultant asked if I understood what he said. In my mind, I just could not comprehend such information and was not accepting that. My husband insisted they resuscitate Isaac once he was born. The doctors said they would not do that as they confirmed he was already dead. They offered their condolence and advised us that I would still have to go ahead and deliver him. I was just waiting to deliver Isaac and take it up from there, expecting a miracle, or perhaps he would be born alive or be raised from the dead.

I was given some drugs to speed up labor and control my blood pressure. Isaac was finally born by forceps delivery at 11:12 a.m. on Monday, May 1. There was

11:12 a.m.

just silence as he was pulled out with the forceps, and the first thing I noticed was his straight, beautiful black hair.

During Antenatal classes, we were told about delivery options. I hoped within me that I would not have to go through a forceps delivery. When I got to the point of delivery, most of my wishes went out. In these situations, you kind of deal with things you are faced with and take the options presented to you at that point in time.

My husband took him from the consultant immediately after he was delivered and began resuscitating him. He continued for some minutes. He prayed fervently in that room with all the doctors and midwives present. I didn't know whether to feel sorry for him or me. I realized that my husband would have laid down his life for our son and what love he had for Isaac.

A FIRST GLIMPSE OF ISAAC

Isaac was wrapped in a blanket and given to me. I was just numb. I first noticed his nose and how much he looked like Charles, even with his eyes closed. I just stared at him. This wasn't how I envisaged our first encounter. My husband told me to give him a kiss; I just kissed him, still in a stunned state. After what seemed like ages, he was taken away for a bath and brought back to us in a Moses Basket. I can't still understand why they stuck a rose in the basket. Did the hospital have to make it obvious he was dead?

I was totally exhausted and lay back in bed. Once in a while, I would lift my head to look at him in the Moses Basket and keep thinking it was not meant to be like this.

Only if he would just stir and cry. Charles, mum, and I were totally quiet. What was there to say? However, each of us had our own thoughts going through our heads. I could not even think far ahead about anything or anyone for that matter. After some hours, my mum suggested they take Isaac away.

The consultant later came round to discuss a few things like funeral arrangements and the post-mortem. Funeral? Never did I imagine I would bury a child of mine in my life. I have always gone past cemeteries and funeral processions and wondered what it was like to lose someone you love. Although I have lost grandparents, it just wasn't the same feeling. Moreover, they were old, and I was not attached to them; hence their demise was bearable for me but not for my parents.

The two options open to us were a joint funeral with other babies (so other babies die and other parents are in the same position as ours, could not comprehend that) or a private funeral which we had to organize

11:12 a.m.

ourselves and pay for. In hindsight, I am so glad we chose to have a private funeral, as we have somewhere to go if we wish, on Isaac's birthday.

It was all too sudden to start thinking about funeral plans, so we asked the hospital for more time to think about it. The consultant discouraged us from having a postmortem as he was quite sure why Isaac died (Placental Abruption), but we were insistent on having one.

One of the midwives who attended to me came in later in the day to see us. While chatting, she informed us that another mum had lost her baby. The child passed away before coming in to the hospital. She didn't feel the baby moving for some time and came in for a check-up. Being the caring person I am, I asked if seeing and encouraging her was okay. What was I thinking? I later realized I had not processed what had happened to me. Fortunately, or unfortunately, she told me that would not be possible as it was confidential information, and she should not have informed us about the other patient in the first place.

Being in a labor ward, you cannot escape the fact that babies do exist. There were cries of newborn babies throughout the day and night. Just hearing their cries made me cry as I would never hear my Isaac cry or get to take him home with me.

I remember all the times I went into the hospital for

Believe

my antenatal appointments and scans and saw proud mums and dads leaving with their babies. I looked forward to my moment, but that was not to be for now.

This is one occasion I sure was glad I was not a man. Charles had to call my family and his family to tell them what had happened. Even after months of losing Isaac, I found it difficult to tell others that my son was dead.

One part of me wanted to run away from that ward to escape my loss, but another wanted to stay there as it was a comfort zone and a reminder that I did have a son. However, I could not leave immediately as I had a blood transfusion (two pints of blood) and was still very weak to get up. This was my first time having a blood transfusion. I was so scared. How do I know if the blood was contamination free or, for that matter, not infected? We were reassured that their blood was screened thoroughly, but we were not totally satisfied. I lost so much blood during labor. There was no alternative to getting my blood supply up immediately, so I had to have the transfusion overnight. Did I sleep? Not at all. I probably thought that if anything were going to happen, it would be better if I was awake and could get help right away, unlike my baby, who died without us having any idea such an occurrence would happen.

On Wednesday, two days after Isaac was born, it was time to go home. Leaving the hospital was the worst day of my life. This was real now. I had lost my baby and

11:12 a.m.

left with High Blood Pressure. As I walked out, I noticed it was a sunny day. It was business as usual for others out there in the world. I felt like hanging a sign over my head saying, I have just lost my baby. Look at me and stop, just as my world had stopped.

By this time, there were a number of messages from other family members and friends on our landline and my mobile to find out if our baby had been born and how we were doing. So, who do you call first? What do you tell them? Was I ready to start explaining what happened? Did I even know what really happened? Was I ready to repeat the same information thirty or more times? All these thoughts went through my head. As I was drained (we got home around 6:00 p.m.), I wanted to go to bed and sleep.

The next few days were spent crying when no one was there so as not to discourage my mum and husband, taking my medication, monitoring my blood pressure, resting, trying to figure out what happened, and asking why me. I looked at pictures of my Isaac, read and reread text messages and cards received, and encouraged myself, mum, dad, and Charles. Some days I just wished I could sleep for ages and not wake up to face my reality.

About a week after Isaac was born, another midwife checked my blood pressure. So far, my BP had been responding to medication. However, on this particular day,

Believe

it had skyrocketed. The midwife advised me to go to my doctor immediately. On getting there, I saw one of the doctors. He was quite alarmed at my BP and indicated I might have a heart attack or stroke. He advised me to go straight back to the same hospital where I lost my baby. I cried all the way to the hospital. I thought, what on earth is going on? Was it not enough that I lost my baby? Would I now have a stroke or heart attack on top of it and maybe die too? Where was God in all of this? "Please, help me," I cried.

We headed straight for the hospital. The staff at the hospital was not happy that the doctor asked me to return to them. I was admitted, and going back there was like reliving the whole experience again. My mum was apprehensive by this time, as we had been away for hours. We all thought it would be a quick visit to the doctor and then back home. I was there for another three nights as my blood pressure was not responding to medication. Once again, my mum stayed with me in hospital. I'm so grateful to have a mum who was there for me. She refused to listen to whatever the midwives said about not being allowed to stay overnight, and she won.

My blood pressure was checked every now and again. During one of such checks, the midwife doing the check asked me where my baby was. I could not believe she asked such a question despite the sticker

11:12 a.m.

on my door signifying I had a stillbirth baby.

Another midwife tried taking my blood. I waited so long for the doctors to do it, and she decided to take it to speed things up so I could go home if the results were fine. But she had no clue what she was doing. It was like a trial-and-error thing. She inserted the needle in the wrong spot, and boy, did I shout or what. Glad when she finally got some blood and was released from such an ordeal. That taught me that I always need to check if medical staff know their jobs well, irrespective of the uniform. I was glad when I was told I could finally go home, focus on my future—not that I had it sorted out, and escape from all the 'bundles of joy' that made my loss harder to bear.

LIFE WITHOUT ISAAC

Whenever I saw a baby on the road or on TV, I cried as I remembered what had happened to me. Sometimes I even wondered if this would happen to me again. Would I get pregnant the second time around? Who could I talk to that would understand what I was going through? It seemed everyone I knew personally had not gone through something similar. However, I learned from conversations afterward that a few friends and relatives had experienced miscarriages.

Believe

I tried to focus by standing on my 'faith,' reading books about women who had challenges with having children and searching the internet non-stop during the day when my mum traveled back home as I had no company because Charles was at work.

> *Who could I talk to that would understand what I was going through?*

I wanted the reassurance that everything would be okay the second time around. The stories I read on the internet were a mixture of sad and happy endings. Sometimes I would log off more discouraged than when I logged in. I remember reading a story of a woman who had thirteen miscarriages. How can someone go through that? I cried for other women as well as myself after reading their stories.

Each time I saw the time read 11:12 a.m., memories of my labor and loss flooded my thoughts. This continued for a long time, and to this day, I still think about Isaac at 11:12 a.m. but with smiles on my face.

I spent some time reflecting on what had happened

11:12 a.m.

and read the book *The Purpose Driven Life* by Rick Warren. This helped me put things into perspective, and it was just timely. This period made me realize I can look ahead with 'faith' despite what happened.

Going out was daunting. I often prayed that I would not come across anyone I knew to avoid talking about Isaac. During the first few months, when I spotted friends from a distance, I just crossed the road and went in the opposite direction. But when I came across friends face to face, I had no choice but to tell them what happened, whether I was ready to talk or not. As time went on, I chose to cherish the nine months we had with Isaac and focus on my tomorrow bringing better things, and I found it a bit easier to deal with talking about our loss. Life, as they say, continues. Isaac was in our minds then and still is. I returned to work, carried on with my usual commitments, and we started thinking about a second baby.

A friend of my husband's recommended we chat with a consultant friend, Mr. J, about what happened to get a neutral medical perspective and address any other issues we had. In September, we called Mr. J and arranged to meet him at the hotel he was staying in for a while on a visit to London. He seemed so warm and approachable. In our discussion, we found out he, too, had lost a young daughter. It made it easier to relate with him. Talking to him brought me loads of encouragement, and he reminded me so much of my dad. What a comfort as my dad was far away. He confirmed some of our fears, indicating that the hospital was most likely negligent when caring for me during labor.

We had a feeling we may be expecting another baby when we visited Mr. J, but as I didn't want to jump to conclusions, I thought it would be better to confirm first and take it up from there. We also discussed future plans and recommendations of hospitals local to us. He promised to recommend a consultant in London whenever we were expecting another baby.

Valentine's Eve

Believe

4

NORTH MIDDLESEX HOSPITAL

As mentioned earlier, I did a lot of reflecting and praying after losing Isaac. I did not want what happened with Isaac ever to happen again. I tried to ensure all areas were covered (physical health, medical advice, getting enough rest, if I had issues with anyone). The two weeks to my next period seemed like ages. I just had that feeling I was pregnant. About a week after seeing Mr. J, we carried out a pregnancy test which Charles purchased as I was reluctant to buy it myself. Charles was present when I did the checking. We waited impatiently to see what the result would be. Whoa, I was pregnant. Things were pretty straightforward forward the second time round. Conception happened the first month we tried. Thank God I did not have to go through a stressful time to conceive.

Valentine's Eve

We were all smiles. Would it be a boy or a girl this time? I preferred a girl as I felt having a boy would bring back too many memories of Isaac. I may fall into the trap of comparing our second son with Isaac, especially when I had no idea what kind of person Isaac would have been.

We considered going private this time as the NHS had let us down—more the hospital in hindsight. After making inquiries, we realized the cost would be a huge commitment, but it would have been worth it. I also found out that some of the consultants in the NHS also work in private hospitals. We figured out that if we had an excellent consultant in the NHS, things would be different this time.

It was time to give Mr. J a call. He was delighted with the news. He recommended an excellent consultant in a hospital in Tooting. After much consideration, I realized it would not be practical for me to go all that way for all my antenatal appointments, especially towards the end of my pregnancy. Ironically, the doctor's name was Isaac too.

We asked Mr. J if he knew of other hospitals nearby with an excellent consultant. After some deliberation, we decided to settle for one of the hospitals in Redbridge. Funny as this consultant's name was Isaac too.

Mr. J passed on my details to the consultant, who actually took the time to call me, which we really

Believe

appreciated. It seemed things were off to a good start. We went to the hospital to register. The receptionist told me they would not accept me at their hospital as I was not resident in the borough. So, my question was, what happened to Choose and Book? It is good to know your rights. We had to stand our ground. Thank God my husband was with me, and we had our way.

By this time, I was between fourteen to fifteen weeks. A first-trimester scan was arranged for me immediately for the following week. That week's wait seemed like forever. We looked eagerly with anticipation for the day. We were hoping it would be twins as compensation for our loss of Isaac. It was a lady sonographer like the first time. She was not too friendly, but I was not bothered by that. All I was interested in was seeing our baby.

After all the usual procedures for the Ultrasound, she blurted out that there was only one baby. Perhaps she read our minds, but we found her attitude rude, probably due to our preconceived desire. Although slightly disappointed, we were glad that at least we had a wonderful baby who seemed healthy. As I was sixteen weeks by this time, I had to return for my twenty-week scan in four weeks.

I concealed my pregnancy this time, especially after our loss. I preferred people not to know I was pregnant till as late as possible.

I planned to leave work very early this time, take

enough rest and just concentrate on having our baby. It was a relief to discover that my blood pressure was stable so far. I was still on blood pressure medication as my doctor and consultant felt it was better to remain on them. In addition, the consultant recommended I take aspirin to help thin my blood and prevent a recurrence of the placental abruption and raised blood pressure. Charles and I were very reluctant about this. After much persuasion and encouragement from my consultant and my own research—not conclusive, as there were arguments for and against, we decided I should take them.

It was just tablets, tablets, and more tablets, every day. I was looking forward to the day I would stop them as I generally do not particularly appreciate taking tablets. I was also on Iron tablets and tried to take Pregnacare a few times. I still don't understand why the Pregnacare tablets must be so big. It's so off-putting. That's why I never stuck to taking them throughout pregnancy.

IT'S A GIRL

Hooray, it was the day for our twenty-week scan. We forgot to buy a copy of the scan at our last ultrasound. This time we went with our change and resolved to go home with a picture of our baby. Did we want to know

Believe

the sex of our baby? Like the first time, if we knew, we may be compelled to tell others the sex of our baby. The sonographer was male this time round. He was very friendly, and we enjoyed our conversation with him. All the checks were done, and everything was fine with our baby—what a relief. We were engrossed in our discussion. We forgot whether we wanted to know our baby's sex. My husband asked him just as he logged out of the main screen what our baby's sex was. He was slightly surprised as he thought we were not keen on knowing. He did a quick check and said he thought it was a girl. As he had other patients waiting, we decided not to push him for confirmation. I was delighted because I had always wanted a girl.

When you hear such news, you just want to shout it. We decided it was time to let the family know. By this time, I had informed my manager at work; she came to me one day and informed me that my colleagues had asked her if I was pregnant. Perhaps they were afraid to ask me directly due to what happened to Isaac. I just wanted to be left alone with no interference. I feel bad now, as I know it was out of concern. I told her to tell them to mind their business jokingly.

My parents, brother, sisters in law, and mother-in-law (she was here then) were over the moon when they heard the news. Two weeks later, friends began to notice and expressed their joy.

Valentine's Eve

On February 13th, 2007, I went to work as usual in my twenty-third week of pregnancy. I only worked two days each week. I managed to get in early at 7:00 a.m. to make up my working hours as I intended to go on annual leave the following week and straight into maternity leave.

Around midday, I felt a slight pain in my tummy. At first, I thought it was nothing. A few hours later, the pain was a bit sharp but for a very short duration. This pain came on and off. It was bearable to an extent, as I consider myself to have a high pain threshold. I felt my daughter move vigorously for about ten seconds. Before this, it was just a thump.

At about 4:50 p.m., I thought I better get another opinion on it but thought it was nothing. I called the hospital there was no response. I rang my husband, who was a bit busy at work but said he would call back, but I should try the hospital again and my consultant. I tried my consultant, who informed me he was abroad. He suggested I keep an eye on the pain and make my way to the hospital if it intensified.

A colleague and friend popped in to see me around 6:00 p.m. She commented that it was great I had come this far and was out of danger regarding the pregnancy. In my mind, I thought I would only be relaxed and with no concern when I delivered my baby, as Isaac was born full term but still died. I decided to continue with work

Believe

and keep an eye on the pain. I was relieved when it was 7:00 p.m., and it was time to go home.

I could not wait to get home as it had been a long day. It took me about one hour to get home. On the way home, the pain came and went. Just as I was approaching home, the pain was a bit stronger. When I walked through the door, my husband was concerned that I was still in pain. He told me to go upstairs and lie down. He brought me dinner in bed. I ate and lay back. The pain just kept on increasing and was more frequent. It got to a point I could not even lie down. I felt the urge to go to the toilet with diarrhea. Then my lower back started to ache badly. It was then that it struck me that it could be labor. We thought that was not possible.

Nevertheless, my husband called '999' and requested an ambulance. When fifteen minutes passed, there was no sign of the ambulance. My husband decided to drive me to the hospital. It was too far to go to the hospital in Redbridge; hence we decided to go to one nearby in North London.

At this point, I was just in constant pain and found it hard to concentrate. I just wanted the pain to stop. I read while researching that labor can be stopped. I was confident that even if it were labor, it would be stopped or delayed with medication. I hurriedly threw a few clothes and toiletries into a bag, and we set off for the hospital.

Valentine's Eve

We finally got to the hospital around 9:30 p.m. My husband banged on the maternity door, but there was no response. He realized that entrance was closed. We went round the corner and were let in. Due to my state, Charles parked right in front of the maternity ward meant for drop-off only and even forgot to switch off his lights, which he discovered the following morning.

We went to the reception desk. There were a few midwives who were busy talking. We informed them I was in pain and might be in labor. When the midwife who took my notes asked how far gone I was and found out I was under twenty-four weeks pregnant, she casually dismissed that I was in labor. I was shown to a room and asked to change into a gown.

We were there for about fifteen minutes; still, no one had come to examine me. My husband was very upset that no one had come to check up on me. He went to the reception desk, gave them a good talking to, and pointed out it was urgent that I was seen as the first hospital was negligent during my first delivery. I placed a cold flannel on my forehead and tummy to relieve the pain as I was feeling very hot.

Then a midwife came in and examined me and said I was about 7 cm dilated and in the late stages of labor. We could not believe I had gone that far. The registrar was called in and informed us that my labor could not be stopped as I had gone too far. I was not expecting

Believe

this as I thought it could and would be stopped. To make matters worse, he said that because our baby would be born extremely premature, they would not resuscitate her as the quality of life of such babies is very poor even if they survive.

All this was a shock. A few hours ago, it was just a typical day, and here I was about to give birth to our baby three months early. My husband refused to agree with their advice and asked to speak to the most senior consultant on duty. He was more sympathetic than the registrar and agreed to do whatever it took to resuscitate the baby. This seemed to calm us down as I was aware that even babies as young as twenty-two weeks could survive, although rare but not impossible. I was given gas and air as a form of pain relief. I blew furiously and continuously to get in the gas and air to cope with the pain I was feeling. One of the midwives had to tell me to slow down. It's hilarious thinking back to how hard I sucked on the mouthpiece. I was left alone to rest and call for attention whenever I felt like pushing.

It was wonderful having my husband as my birthing partner. He helped massage my back which seemed like it was set on fire. After some time, I felt like pushing. My husband ran out to call them. A team of midwives and doctors, including the consultant, came in. The pushing bit was not easy. I finally managed to push our baby girl out.

Valentine's Eve

She was born at 11:23 p.m. on February 13. She weighed 500 g. She looked tiny from where I lay in bed. She was put into an incubator, and the doctors worked on her. The hospital rang Homerton Hospital so she could be transferred there as they have a specialist unit for pre-term babies. We were told everything was looking good and she would be transferred shortly. I was very exhausted after this and dozed off. When I woke up, I was told the ambulance was on its way to pick Faith up. Charles decided to call her Faith on the spot as he had been studying that theme in recent weeks. I liked the name, and it was also something to hold on to that 'Faith' would make it.

MATTER OF LIFE AND DEATH

The Ambulance team from Royal London Hospital arrived to take her over to Homerton Hospital. She was taken to a room where the incubator and other equipment were set up to monitor her oxygen levels. Charles informed me of the latest developments, and I went to sleep confident that our Faith would be fine.

After a few hours, Charles sat on an armchair, red-eyed and exhausted. I asked for an update, expecting she was already in Homerton. I was told the team was trying to stabilize her oxygen level (I think that was what it was) and would not be able to take her until that was sorted. I was not expecting such news as things seemed to be looking good. However, I was still confident it would be okay. Moreover, I had been assured by spiritual mentors that what happened to Isaac would never happen again.

Although having a pre-term baby would be challenging and unplanned, it was better for me than having no baby. My husband was shuffling between Faith and me. Around 5:00 a.m. in the morning, I went to see Faith. She looked so long and thin. There were tubes everywhere. I was not sure what I was expecting but what mattered was that she survived. Despite the tubes, she looked very beautiful. We were told the oxygen levels were dropping rapidly, and she was in a lot of pain. I stood there watching the oxygen readings and praying. As a parent, you would not want your child to be in pain. We just prayed and believed a miracle would occur. I spoke to Faith, and said you need to make it and pull through.

A SECOND LOSS

After an hour or so, things were still looking bad. They took a scan of Faith's brain, and we were told she had suffered some brain damage and we should consider letting her go. How could we let her go? She was a source of consolation after the loss of Isaac. We were adamant they should give her all the help available, and we still believed in a miracle.

Sometime later, the consultant sat us down and explained that there was not much they could do and that we should let her go. I could not believe we were actually having such a conversation. One loss was more than enough. O God, not two, please. While we were still deliberating on the next course of action, a nurse came in and whispered something in the consultant's ear. He then told us she did not have long to live and that we should go in and say our goodbyes.

I felt bewildered, just as with Isaac. Even to the last second, I was still very hopeful. She was taken out of the incubator and handed to me. Charles carried her, and then I carried her. And she was gone. I could not even cry. Twenty fours ago, it was a completely different story. I sat in a hospital with our baby in my arms. She was still meant to be in my tummy, protected in my womb and still growing.

How could we let her go?
Even to the last second, I was
still very hopeful.

Believe

We later handed her over to a midwife for a bath. We went back to a room for parents (at least the room was much more pleasant than a hospital room) and sat there in total silence. Faith was later brought to us.

I peeped at her from time to time in the Moses basket placed on the center table. The clothes she had on were very tiny, probably smaller than a doll's. I remember regretting that I didn't cradle Isaac in my arms when he died. I just did not have the strength to cuddle Faith even the second time round.

I was supposed to go to work that morning. I rang my manager and said I would not be at work but would keep her informed. How can my second baby die? How was I to convey that to others?

After many hours we said our goodbyes to Faith. Where was she taken to? How did she feel there? Well, I knew Faith had gone. It was just her physical body left behind. I told her she was loved so much and looked forward to seeing her in Heaven.

I was then transferred to a room with a double bed. As I lay on the bed, I thought and said to Charles, "I cannot do this again—go through another pregnancy." The hospital staff did their best; we knew it was just out of their hands.

All sorts of thoughts went through my head. Did I not learn a lesson I should have learned the first time? Who really was responsible for all these calamities that had befallen me? Is motherhood not for me? Were we being punished for something we had done or our parents/family had done?

I could not go through the emotional trauma I went through with Isaac. I just said, God, I accept it if this is your will. I was later discharged on the evening of February 14 (Valentine's Day). We were too tired to celebrate the day and not in this circumstance. Anyway, we got around to exchanging our gifts. Charles rustled up some dinner; we ate and went to bed.

The next day was the day to start dealing with our loss. We rang my brother, sister in laws, and mother-in-law and told them what happened. They were astonished, and all rushed to our house. They spent the whole day with us, which helped me take my mind off things. We decided not to tell my parents until the weekend so as not to disrupt their plans for the week.

This was one of the hardest things I had ever done. Charles broke the news to my dad. His first comment was, "It has happened again." These words were etched in my memory for a long time, and I prayed this would never be said of me again. I spoke to him right after and had to encourage him. Faith was the second grandchild he had lost. I told him to convey the news to my mum as I knew she would be overwhelmed with such news.

My dad passed the phone to my mum, and there was panic in her voice. She asked me what was going on.

Believe

I was quite surprised by her question and asked if my dad had told her. She replied, "Told me what?" How do I break the news to her? I told her, and she screamed and cried. It was too much for her to take in. I needed encouragement at this point in my life, but I had to be the encourager.

I spent a week resting and decided I would not be beaten, feel sorry for myself, or let my loss destroy me. I decided to focus on my future. Faith had a very quiet funeral with just the two of us present. We were asked if we had any flowers to lay on her grave. Amid everything we forgot. I cried because I realized I would not find her favorite color, toys, or what she would have liked or disliked. My only consolation was that we would meet sometime again in the future when there would be no more tears.

We had initially planned a few weeks before Faith was born to attend a baby show in London. We bought the tickets and were looking forward to the baby show. Before the show's commencement, faith was born premature and did not make it. We could either go for the show or not go for the show. I refused to let Faith's death cripple me. In addition, I was not going to waste the money we spent on those tickets (just joking). It was important to me that we went for the show as a sign of faith and that we would hold our own babies and take them home with us someday soon.

Valentine's Eve

As it was a baby show, you could not avoid questions like do you have any children? Are you expecting any children? In the natural, the only reason you would attend a show like that is that you have a child(ren) or are expecting one. I mumbled something along the lines of we were just looking around or planning ahead.

I refused to let Faith's death cripple me.

There was a stand with midwives providing advice. My husband suggested we go over and chat with them. I knew that going there would mean opening up and disclosing my whole pregnancy history. Was I in the mood for this? Charles insisted and said who knows? We may get some beneficial advice. I reluctantly agreed. The ladies were very sympathetic and supportive and referred us to some websites for further information and offered some suggestions on the way forward. One of the ladies also said I would hopefully be lucky the third time round.

Not long after this, I began to feel broody, and we thought of trying again. Isaac and Faith will forever be in our minds.

Christmas Eve

Believe

5

THIRD TIME BLESSED

It has been a year (May 1, 2007) since Isaac left us. It was a bit somber as we stood at his graveside. We were here to reflect on the year that had gone by without Isaac. There were a few tears in recognition of our temporal separation but gladness in light of our future reunion.

Ironically, although we were there for Isaac, Faith could not be left out as she, too, was lain to rest there. But as it was Isaac's day, I focused more on Isaac. As I stood there, it dawned on me that my past, present, and future were intertwined. My past loss, Isaac, my present loss, Faith, and my future gain, my third baby, were all there at the Chingford Cemetery.

We were one hundred percent sure that without a pregnancy test (let's say we had a witness within

Christmas Eve

us), I was pregnant by this date, although I still had two weeks to know for sure. I was glad the next two weeks flew by so quickly. Charles decided he wanted to be in the frontline this time around. He took my urine sample and proceeded with the test. For some reason, he did not want me to look as he wanted to break the news to me himself.

We were elated when the test showed positive. I just prayed that the outcome would be different this time around and that there would be no complications. After the news sunk in, I realized this would be pregnancy (journey) number three.

On May 25, 2007, we had an appointment with Ms. AA (consultant for Faith) to discuss the postmortem result for Faith. This date is so special as it is my only sister's birthday and the day Isaac was buried. Here we sat in Ms. AA's office discussing what led to Faith's death. Well, the postmortem gave no apparent reason why she died. Perhaps I might have felt better if there was a reason.

On the other hand, if there were a reason, the temptation would be there to get upset that such a thing caused her death. What had happened had happened. The only thing I can control is my response to the events that had occurred. Although brief, I chose to cherish the times I had with my children and look expectantly to my future.

Believe

We decided to tell Ms. AA the good news about my pregnancy. She was overjoyed for us. Actually, she was the first person we told as we wanted to do everything in our power to ensure I got appropriate medical attention. She talked briefly about what I could expect regarding procedures but said she would go into more detail when the time was right. We left her office trusting that she was an answer to prayer and that things would turn out differently this time.

We decided to set things in motion quickly. I booked an appointment with my doctor. He was so glad to hear I was pregnant. I specifically requested that he indicate on the referral form to the hospital that I wanted Ms. AA as my consultant. The papers were sent off, and I had to wait for the hospital to contact me.

When I was about ten weeks pregnant, we were all set for church. I felt a very sharp pain in my tummy. At first, I thought nothing of it, but the pain was still persistent. My husband thought it was worth checking it out. I headed for the hospital. I gave Ms. AA a quick call, and she suggested I go straight to A & E, and she would leave a message for the doctor in charge to attend to me. I waited a bit before I was seen at the hospital. Checks were done, and the doctor who attended to me advised me that nothing was wrong and that I should just rest. I felt cared for and looked after. I was just glad it was not a miscarriage or some other complication.

Christmas Eve

TWINS OR MORE, LORD!

The following week I had a follow-up appointment booked to see my consultant. It was nice seeing her again. After the routine checks and some questions, she decided to do an ultrasound on the spur of the moment. I was not prepared for that. Moreover, Charles was not with me. We had been looking forward to our first ultrasound. It would be our first opportunity to meet our babies. We kind of prayed we would have at least twins, considering the loss we had. Also, it would mean no rush to have more babies after this or perhaps no more babies, and I would be free from the demand pregnancy places on a woman.

Ms. AA wanted to reassure herself and me that everything was fine with the baby. Well, a pleasant surprise won't hurt, I thought. I braced myself as she placed the joystick on my tummy and awaited the news of twins. She turned the screen and broke the silence, and said congratulations.

She had this unique smile and wink that made me relax and trust that things would turn out fine. That wink and smile were very encouraging throughout my pregnancy.

I was jolted from my daydream and looked at the tiny outline of my baby. I was excited that I had a baby (even though it was not babies) that seemed fine at this moment.

Believe

She even went ahead and printed a picture for me for free. Hopefully, that would serve as compensation for Charles, who missed this opportunity. He was glad we had a baby.

I was back at the hospital for my twelve-week ultrasound in two weeks, and Charles gladly accompanied me. All the checks and measurements were done, and the baby was doing great. I had not been booked in for this pregnancy, so Ms. AA asked the head midwife to do that quickly. Each time I saw a midwife in the hospital or went for numerous scans, I had to tell the midwife, doctor, or sonographer why I was in the hospital, coming for another check-up, or having another scan. The midwife that took my details was friendly, and I felt comfortable around her. She asked for my personal details and that of Charles. She recorded the information I provided in my hospital book. She also wanted information about my previous pregnancies. I then had to recount all that had happened to me. If only that were the end, but it wasn't. I could not help the tears that rolled down my eyes as I talked about the loss of my two children.

It makes me wonder what the essence is for taking notes. I guess medical personnel are either too busy or can't be bothered to read the notes. It seems they are oblivious to the strain the constant repetition of one's unfortunate history can have on an individual. It got to a point I had to detach myself from the sad aspects of my past obstetric history; otherwise, I would have suffered from depression. There was no room for gloominess.

CAN HE & WILL HE?

In the middle of the questioning, the midwife asked me, "Do you believe in God?" I did not anticipate such a question. Of course, I believed in God, but I interpreted the question to mean, did I believe in God to see me through this pregnancy and deliver my baby safe and sound.

The answer to that question at that point in time was no. My belief in God was so battered that I felt that if He allowed me to lose two children despite our prayers and hope in him, what guarantee did I have that things would be okay the third time?

Needless to say, I felt ashamed that I had this attitude, but that was what went on in my mind subconsciously. I told Charles about my discussion with the midwife, and he pointed out that my faith was low and needed to be built up.

The midwife offered me the triple test, which I declined. But she left it open in case I changed my mind. I just had this weird feeling that if I took the test, the markers would come out high, and I would be told there was a high chance I may have a Down syndrome child and probably asked to consider termination.

Maybe my feeling was wrong, but I just chose not to go along with the test, and moreover, I never did the test in the previous two pregnancies.

TO STITCH OR NOT TO STITCH?

My consultant advised me to have a cervical stitch because my second baby was born prematurely. This will prevent my cervix from opening early and prevent premature birth. There was no guarantee, though, and the procedure carried a high risk of miscarriage or infection. I was in a dilemma. If I did nothing, I could have another premature birth with no guarantee that our baby would make it.

On the other hand, if I went ahead with the procedure, there would be a slight risk of a miscarriage, premature birth, or infection. I was so confused. We kept on stalling on making this decision.

I prayed about it but didn't get a definitive answer. I even asked my midwife for advice, but she indirectly suggested it was my decision. I read up on this procedure, and there were more points against the procedure than for it. Time was running out, and by week sixteen, I had to let my consultant know our decision, as this is

Christmas Eve

the time limit to carry out the procedure. We decided to go ahead with it and felt at peace. I chose to do the procedure on a Friday to give me enough time to rest over the weekend.

Different consultants carry out a 'cervical stitch' procedure on certain days of the week. I dreaded the 17th of July, 2007. I was very disappointed that my consultant was not the one to carry out the procedure when I told her of my proposed date. Anything could go wrong. What if I reacted to the drugs I was given or had a miscarriage while in theatre? I just had to shut out all these thoughts and focus on the end goal of having a 'bouncing' baby.

I just had to shut out all these thoughts and focus on the end goal of having a 'bouncing' baby.

The day finally arrived. I went into the hospital around 8:00 a.m. I was allocated to a room and told to change into a hospital gown. My consultant came in to say hello and to see how I was doing. She informed me

Believe

I would be taken into the theatre shortly. One hour, two hours, three hours went. She returned several times to apologize as there were a few emergencies that day, and the theatre was in constant use.

Finally, one of the anesthetists came in and explained what was to happen in the theatre. As already agreed with Ms. AA, Charles was supposed to go into the theatre with me. As we approached the theatre entrance, Charles was told this was how far he could go, and he would have to stay behind in the waiting room. We could not believe what we were told. There was no time even to argue. I was wheeled in immediately.

I was transferred to the bed, asked a few questions, and the spinal block commenced. This was my first time inside a theatre; there were about five people in there. It was a bit scary. I really needed Charles in there. It then dawned on me that I needed God more than ever. Was it a coincidence that the song playing in the theatre was something like trusting in God? I am not even sure if the staff there were Christians or not.

Once the spinal block was administered, both my legs went limp. It was a very strange feeling. I tried to move my legs but just could not get them to move. After the spinal block, I had to lie back and wait for the consultant to turn up. I was very frustrated as I wanted the whole thing to be over. I had not eaten all day. However, this was the least of my worries. I'd been waiting from

Christmas Eve

8:00 a.m. for the procedure, and when I eventually got into the theatre at about 3:00 p.m., I still had to wait for the cervical stitch to be done. Eventually, the consultant turned up with the registrar.

At first, I thought he was just pointing out to the registrar how the procedure was done, but to my horror, the registrar carried out the procedure under the direction of the consultant. Should I complain? My consultant had told me that only consultants carried out a cervical stitch procedure. I thought, "My life is in the balance here! What if something goes wrong?" I just continued praying that all would go well. I was relieved when it was all over. I was wheeled back to the room I was in previously.

After an hour, I was offered something to eat — what a relief. I was told the anesthetic would take a few hours to wear off. After about two hours, my legs were still numb. I began to wonder what if I became paralyzed. Or could it be that I reacted to the drugs, and I would never be able to walk again? I had to dispel such thoughts and hoped nothing of that nature happened to me. Eventually, the drugs wore off, and I could lift my leg gradually and walk. Thank God for that.

At around 8:00 p.m., I was transferred to a women's ward in a different department of the hospital. The majority of the women in there had gynecology issues. I had something to eat and, after an hour, slept off.

Believe

I decided not to take my bath in the morning as I expected to be discharged. While brushing my teeth, one of the ladies asked me if I had lost my baby. In my mind, I confessed that would not happen to me. I smiled and said no. After all, I had been through, baby number three was here to stay.

As usual, it took a long time before the doctors came for their ward rounds. I was elated when he said it was okay to go home. Charles came to pick me up on Saturday evening, and we headed home. I ensured the next seven days were spent resting and doing 'little' housework. You just can't avoid it, especially if you are female and a 'perfectionist.'

MY SECOND HOME

The hospital became my second home. I had scans booked every four weeks from my twentieth week until delivery. I was very anxious during this period because I did not want to hear any unexpected news that my cervix was opening prematurely or that something was wrong with our baby. Happy to say that none of my concerns were valid.

From my thirty-second week, I began to visit the hospital twice a week, Maternity Day Unit (MDU), for a check-up to ensure any danger signs were picked

Christmas Eve

up immediately and both myself and baby were doing fine. The check-up was an all-day affair. Although I had an appointment, the midwives usually ran late and shuttled between the labor ward and the MDU, where checks were carried out.

During one of such visits in my thirty-third week of pregnancy, part of my monitoring consisted of monitoring my baby's heartbeat. I had been in bed for close to an hour, and I was really exhausted and couldn't wait to leave. I was waiting for one of the midwives to show up and take me off. All of a sudden, I didn't hear my baby's heartbeat. At first, I thought I must have imagined it, as it is quite common for other babies' heartbeats to be louder than one's own.

To be sure I didn't imagine things, I cast my eyes over to the tracing machine and noticed there was a huge dip. I called out to the midwife, no response. Then I yelled, "Can someone please get me the midwife?" While I was considering taking the belt off my tummy and getting the midwife myself, she came in. Still in a panicked state, I told her to check the trace; she had a worried look on her face. This just scared me. I had to restrain myself from shouting. She was quite calm and asked me to lie on my side. She tried to find the baby's heartbeat but had no luck. She asked me to roll over to the other side, and still no heartbeat. By this time, I could not restrain myself. I began to say

Jesus and was nearly in tears. In my mind, all I could think of was to get me straight to the theatre. My baby must not die! I had come too far for this!

NOT NOW, PLEASE

The midwife pressed the bell (probably an emergency one) and shouted, 'can I get some help in here!' Before I knew what was happening, there was two medical staff, and I was asked to sit in a wheelchair and overheard them saying I was going straight to the theatre. It felt like a dream. Some minutes ago, I was nearly dozing off, and the baby's heart was tugging away, and the next minute there was no heartbeat, and I was going to have an emergency cesarean. I always prayed that it would never come to that. At that point, the main thing was to have my baby alive, even if it meant a cesarean. I dialed my husband and asked him to come immediately as it seemed our baby's heart had stopped beating. Poor Charles, he drove like 'mad' to the hospital. He was actually having his lunch when I called; he lost his appetite entirely on hearing such news.

I was taken into a side room to be prepared for theatre and asked to change into a hospital gown. I thought to myself, why is time being wasted? Get me in there. My consultant was glad because I had come

Christmas Eve

quite far the previous week and said she wouldn't be too worried if my baby arrived. I gave her a quick call to inform her of what was happening. She had told me to call her if anything happened or if I had concerns of any sort.

She said she was in the hospital and would see me right away. She was with me in less than three minutes. I was so relieved to see her. She was quite upset that no one had informed her about my situation. She immediately took charge and asked them to hold on with the medicine I was to take in readiness for the procedure. She asked if I was shown my baby's heartbeat, and I said no. As I had taken my spectacles off during all the panic, I popped them back on, and I was shown my baby's heartbeat on the monitor and heard his heartbeat. At first, it was very faint, and then it became very loud and consistent. Phew!

The monitor was kept on for about two hours to keep an eye on my baby. Charles arrived and was glad to learn that baby and I were doing great. I informed my consultant that I wanted to stay the night to ensure I was in the right place to prevent anything of that nature from happening again. She obliged my request. I kept a close eye on the clock to ensure all observations recommended by my consultant were adhered to by the midwives at the right time. The following day I was discharged.

Believe

The next four weeks were literally spent in and out of the hospital. I was there at least three times a week. I was looking forward to my thirty-seventh week. By this time, the baby would be full term and ready to be welcomed into our world.

We decided to remove the stitch (placed in by the seventeenth week of pregnancy) on the 21st of December. I was told I could go into labor immediately after removing the stitch. Well, I didn't, thank God. I wasn't just ready. Charles wanted a pre-Christmas baby; I wanted a post-Christmas baby. On the morning of the 23rd, we went to church as usual. I was in constant pain throughout the service and the whole day (although the pain was mild). I tried to rest when I got home and left the housework for another day.

THE HEBREW WOMAN EXPERIENCE

On Monday, it was the same thing. However, around 6:00 p.m. in the evening, the pain became stronger and more consistent. By 7:00 p.m., we thought it was a good idea to get my consultant's opinion. She advised me to go to the hospital if the contractions came every five minutes. After thirty minutes of continuous pain with no respite, we headed for the hospital.

We were told to wait in a waiting room, and after about thirty minutes, I was called into an assessment

Christmas Eve

room. My urine and blood pressure were checked, and the baby was monitored. The pain intensified, and my eyes were glued to the tracings to ensure my baby was fine. Around 9:30 p.m., I was taken off the machine, and the midwife told me nothing was happening, and no midwife would be excited about the trace as the baby was relaxed and still holding on tight to his womb environment. A doctor came in later on and carried out a physical examination. She informed me that the neck of my womb was still closed, but to be on the safe side, she would like to keep me overnight. Well, it was good she said that as I was not planning to leave that hospital that night due to the pain I felt, and I wanted to be in the hospital just in case.

Just before 10:00 p.m., I felt the urge to use the toilet. I had a runny stool (diarrhea), and it crossed my mind that perhaps labor had started, but I thought not due to the doctor's findings. Suddenly, it seemed the pain ascended to a great height. I couldn't sit, stand, or talk. It intensified with each passing minute. I returned to the room and awaited a transfer upstairs, where I would spend the night. I asked Charles to get me a midwife right away.

She arrived within a few minutes and asked me what the problem was. I explained that I was in a lot of pain and felt like pushing. I felt silly saying, how can I want to push when baby isn't due yet? She wanted me to lie down so she could examine me. I thought, lie down! At this point, I was in pain all over. I managed somehow to lie down with incredible difficulty. She examined me and informed me she could feel the baby's head. I couldn't believe my ears; you mean I was in labor? The bed wasn't the right bed for labor. Charles had to help a bit as things happened so fast. The pushing wasn't easy. If you have been there, you know what I am talking about. Our baby was pulled out in less than thirty minutes with one final push. He didn't make a sound. I thought, give me a sign you are okay. Perhaps he heard me. He spluttered and coughed. He was born at 10:30 p.m. on December 24, 2007, weighing 5 pounds and 7 ounces.

MY OWN BABY

So, it finally happened! Many thoughts ran through my head, the anxiety of the last thirty-seven weeks. The fears of the past, the hitches along the way, the prayers made and all the visits to the hospital. Whoa, we made it. I now have a baby to hold and take home. When he was placed in my arms, what a wonderful feeling. Words cannot describe that moment. I couldn't take my eyes off him. He was beautiful, and I'm not saying it because I am his mother. We called my brother and sisters-in-law. They were over the moon. One of my sisters-in-law

Christmas Eve

screamed when she heard the news. A baby boy! I burst into tears, realizing the impact of the journey of the last two years.

So, it finally happened! I now have a baby to hold and take home.

I was quite exhausted but managed to doze off now and again. Each time I opened my eyes, I leaned over and checked to ensure he was still breathing (I wonder if all new mums do that). Three midwives came in as early as 6:00 a.m. to say congratulations when they saw my name on the board. They had cared for me in the last five weeks in my numerous visits to the MDU. They were very thrilled for me. I couldn't have asked for a better Christmas present.

GOD DID IT AGAIN

Two years after the birth of our second son, we decided to try for baby number four. I conceived within a few months. This journey was much easier because

Believe

our previous pregnancy resulted in a live birth. I wasn't taking any chances, however. I meditated on God's word, prayed, and stayed under the care of Miss AA, my fantastic consultant. As with my third pregnancy, I went through the same procedure.

Based on my history, I was closely monitored, and as my pregnancy progressed, I had weekly appointments in the MDU. On one of my scans, I was advised that my baby would likely be born with Down Syndrome. We were offered a test to determine this. As we didn't plan to terminate the baby, we opted out of this test and had to wait it out. The pregnancy went well. At thirty-seven weeks plus, our fourth baby and third son were born. He was born perfectly healthy.

Paradigm Shift

Believe

6

FUNKE, FOLKS & FAITH

In this chapter, I would like to share my thoughts, agony, questions, and response with you during the loss of Isaac and Faith.

Prior to losing my first and second child, I had not experienced and fully comprehended the effect of losing someone you love and cherish so much. Although I had lost my maternal grandfather and paternal grandmother, although saddened, it didn't have a significant impact on me as I was not that close to them, and I considered them to be well advanced in years.

Being a private person, I have always learned to deal with my troubles independently. It was the day of Isaac's funeral that it sunk in and I kind of accepted

Paradigm Shift

that Isaac was permanently separated from us. It took a while for it to sink in that Isaac was really gone, and he was not coming back — I had prayed and hoped for a miracle, i.e., he would be raised from the dead.

As we laid Isaac to rest, I refused to take part in covering his coffin with earth. I could not bring myself to enter the hearse from the funeral directors (I insisted we drive our own car) as I felt that would mean death had won. I could not believe that I was actually burying my own son.

The following months were challenging. Everywhere I went, some things I saw reminded me of my Isaac. Whenever I saw a baby, a pregnant woman, or anyone named Isaac, I remembered that Isaac should not have died. Anytime I went past the cemetery where Isaac was laid to rest, I remembered him, which was very often as the cemetery is close to where I live, I got mailings in the post from Pampers in respect of Isaac (they were unaware he passed away in the womb shortly before he was born).

I needed time and space to make sense of what had happened to me. Sometimes people did not understand why I needed space and were actually offended when I requested they defer their visits. When people called and offered words of encouragement, sometimes it made me cry, sometimes angry. They had no clue what I was experiencing, but sometimes, their soothing words offered me a glimmer of hope. I remember going to a party some months after Isaac's demise, and a friend said, 'don't worry, God will give you another child.' As far as I was concerned, another child was not the issue. The issue was, why did Isaac have to die? Moreover, another child was another child and not Isaac.

> *I needed time and space to make sense of what had happened to me.*

The turning point came for me after hearing a phrase from a message at church; God is not your problem. I was liberated and realized that I had subconsciously been angry with God for all my misfortune.

Now I could trust him unreservedly and believe my future was bright and colorful and I would get there.

I had to build my confidence in the living God who alone could help me. I was aware that as a result of the experience of losing two babies, I needed an alternative experience that would cause me to believe that the impossible was possible.

I found this alternative in God's word (Bible). I searched through the scriptures and recorded God's thoughts towards me, my well-being, and his plans for me regarding childbirth in a diary.

The truth I found set me free, and I pray that you will get answers and experience God's presence, peace, and hope as you search.

BAD THINGS HAPPEN TO GOOD PEOPLE TOO

Fourteen days after Isaac was born and died, I decided to spend some time studying, reflecting, and trying to understand the situation I found myself in. I read the book of Job. Interestingly, we went through a forty-day journey around that time using the Purpose Driven Life. Some days I felt okay; I recognized what had happened and perhaps why. On other days I just could not understand why it had to happen and why it had to happen to me. My doctor told me that in her twenty-plus years of practice, she had not encountered anyone who had experienced a placental abruption. It was more so annoying when I discovered that placental abruptions are more likely to occur in women who smoke. I had never smoked, so why me?

At the end of my forty-day meditation, I concluded that God was in control, although I did not have all the answers. This would never happen again after applying

Believe

the medical advice given and praying against a repetition. Our friend said we did not deserve to lose our son because he felt we were good people. On the outside, people may look good based on their character or perhaps personalities, but in reality, no one is good in his own strength or based on his ability. Our goodness comes from us accepting God and He making us righteous.

In hindsight, I do not wish the loss of a child on anyone, no matter how bad I think they may be. This is something others have echoed who have been in my shoes.

I believe bad things happen for several reasons; this list is not conclusive. These are based on the fact that we live in a sinful world. Other people's actions bring these about, in some instances, our choices, the devil our adversary, and sometimes it is a time of testing or trials. Hence every human being would experience bad things at some point in their lives.

BUSINESS AS USUAL

I dreaded going back to work. I just didn't know what to expect. I sure was glad to have my old desk back (familiar surroundings) and just get straight to work. One of my colleagues whom I had not met (she had

Paradigm Shift

been off for a while before joining the section) had the audacity to ask me if my baby was a boy or a girl. I was gobsmacked.

First and foremost, she did not know me, and we had no relationship whatsoever. Secondly, what did it matter? My son was dead. Whether my baby was a boy or a girl made no difference.

Another friend who worked on a different floor apparently had not heard about the loss of my son. She was happy to see me and asked after my baby. She commented that they must be very big now. I then had to explain that my baby had died. After these incidences, I settled into work as it was business as usual.

Before my first pregnancy, people who knew me wanted to know if we had any children. We often responded, not yet. After losing Isaac and Faith, when I was asked if I had any children by acquaintances or people I had just met, I was sometimes taken aback, especially if I was not expecting the question. I responded in several ways depending on my mood or the enquirer. My response was along these lines; not at the moment, no, em em yes, no, it's a long story, I had two, but I lost them. Anytime I gave a response that referred to Isaac and Faith, there was a silence that brought on an uncomfortable air. To deal with this, I usually changed the topic, especially when I did not feel like discussing what had happened to me.

Believe

THE LORD IS WITH ME

Although the Bible says God will never leave nor forsake his children, I totally felt abandoned by God, especially after Isaac. I could not help but wonder what some people may have thought, "After all, she is a Christian, and such a terrible thing happened to her." How could God have been with me, and such terrible things occurred in my life? With time—many months later- I realized that how I felt did not change the fact that God was with me. Three different experiences made me doubtless that God was with me throughout this phase of my life. He knew what would happen before it did and prepared me, although I was totally clueless at that point. I will share two of these with you.

I remember I was in the toilet a few weeks before Isaac was due. It's interesting that I hear God a lot here, probably because my mind is not working at its usual rate of twenty thoughts per minute, not that I calculated it, and He dropped a thought in my mind. When unexpected events happen, people will always believe that if the situation had been otherwise when the catastrophe took place, then the tragedy would not have occurred. In addition, they blame themselves or others for making the choice they made, for instance, to go out that day, take a particular bus instead of another or walk a particular path at night. On the one hand, if the person had made a different choice, things may not have turned out differently.

I have always thought how wonderful it would be if we could just see the alternative situation, just like in the Sliding Doors film starring Gwyneth Paltrow and John Hannah in 1998. In most cases, we do not have that insight, and the film still leaves the audience to speculate about the outcome. On the other hand, it does not mean that whatever happened may not have happened at some point in the future, even if the situation was totally different.

I thought, what an interesting thought, and left it there. Only months later, it dawned on me that the conversation was about Isaac's death. The thought brought me a lot of comfort and averted a lot of self-torment as I had so many 'only if' scenarios playing in my mind and wished things had just been different and it did not end up the way it did. I knew I had to work through my pain and receive God's comfort, healing, and encouragement from those He brought my way.

The second experience was linked with my trip to the Philippines in August 2001. It was a Mission trip organized by Tearfund, a Christian charity working to alleviate poverty and tackle the world's challenges, especially in developing countries. We visited a number of local projects to find out what they did. One such project was an orphanage where we spent a few days teaching

Believe

the children and got involved in their sports day and talent show. We got our hands dirty and discovered more about the Filipino people and their culture.

We were also privileged to attend the fortieth anniversary of Christian Growth Ministry, the main sponsor of the orphanage. During this occasion, as we worshipped, the Lord laid a word on my heart concerning Jeremiah chapter one. There He told Jeremiah He knew him before he was formed in his mother's womb. He sanctified him before he was born and called him to be a prophet unto the nations. Immediately I thought the Lord was calling me to do a great work for Him.

I cried and surrendered myself to whatever call He had in store for me. It was only in 2009 that God reminded me of the Filipino incident and pointed out that the revelation was not about me but my second son. I was dumbfounded to think that He knew that I would go through all I went through and provided the answer to my prayers even before I got married, conceived, lost Isaac, lost Faith, and wondered if I would ever be a mum again. Whoa, it just blew my mind. We often say that as Christians, God has already made a provision even before the need arises. This just demonstrated it to me like never before. So, I should have no difficulty trusting Him again. I need to focus on the word. Otherwise, it would be easy to sink like

Peter when he took his eyes off Jesus and considered the turbulent waves.

MORE HARM THAN GOOD

I have realized that if you have not experienced the loss of a loved one, you cannot understand what those affected are going through. In addition, the loss experienced will differ from person to person based on their relationship with the deceased person. Lastly, the fact that I have experienced the loss of a loved one does not mean I necessarily understand what the other bereaved person is going through, as the circumstances or impact may be totally different from my own experience. Based on these and other realizations, I found some comments from people to be unhelpful, shocking, and painful. Having said this, I know some comments are well-meaning and have no intention of hurting the bereaved. I remember our friend lost his child some years before we lost our babies. Although I didn't know what to say, I felt I had to say something and cringe when I remember what I had said to him. Although there was some truth in it, it may not have been the ideal time to offer such comfort.

Below are some comments I found unhelpful when grieving Isaac's loss.

Believe

"Don't worry. You can have another baby."

At that point in time, another baby was not in the equation. I had waited sixteen months to conceive Isaac, gone through nine months of eager anticipation for my own baby, and all of a sudden, he was gone, and all I was expected to do was think of the fact I could have another child.

People called many months after Isaac's death, although they were informed, and made excuses on why they could not call earlier. Although there were some days I would ignore calls because I just was not up to crying again. Condolence messages triggered tears. The fact that I got a call indicated that this person cared, and they took time out of their everyday lives to brighten my shattered one. At times people sent text messages as they were 'scared' to call, which I appreciated and read and reread, especially when I was really down or wanted to convince myself it was not a dream. Isaac was truly gone. On other occasions, people had no clue what to say. Although the silence was awkward, I knew they cared, which did not bother me. The situation was equally awkward for me too.

"Perhaps he was not meant to be."

Even if that was the case, I don't think it is appropriate, especially if the person saying such a thing has children or has not experienced the loss of a baby.

Paradigm Shift

"I know how you feel."

As explained earlier, it is unhelpful to compare one's experience with the experience of one who is recently bereaved. In my own experience, how I feel about my children's loss is totally different from how I felt three years ago. So, I cannot tell someone who is bereaved now that I know how they feel. All I can do is be there for them and be sympathetic.

A friend, bless his soul, sent a detailed email round to others to say I had lost my baby; not sure how he got that information, and the interesting thing was he had not even called to express his condolence. Perhaps he spoke to my husband and included me on the mailing list. I was furious but had to 'forgive' him as that was the least of my worries then.

"God has a purpose for this."

I could not see the purpose in my baby dying. It did not make sense, and as far as I was concerned, it should not have happened. Even if there was a purpose for my pain, such a comment is not ideal in a time of mourning.

"You had a miscarriage which is not as bad as a full-term baby."

I found this very upsetting as Faith was born premature and alive. Also, in the case of Isaac, someone

Believe

referred to the fact that he wasn't full term, so my loss should not be great, which he was. This thinking probably stems from the fact that such people think a baby is not a person. Hence their demise should not matter. It does not matter whether the baby was born premature or full term. The fact remained that from the day I conceived all my babies, they had identities, I spoke to them, and they were human, not mere fetuses.

"Perhaps he would have had difficulties (i.e., health, behavioral) later in life; so, it was better he went now."
Despite challenges, most mothers would still love and want their children.

"Time heals."
I am of the opinion that God heals.

"What happened?"
I can't recount the number of times I had to tell the same sad tale repeatedly. It made me angry in the early days just thinking Isaac's life was just wasted due to a failure in the duty of care by the hospital. Although people asked out of concern, the impact was huge on me.

Paradigm Shift

AM I PARANOID OR WHAT?

Growing up in an African background, I could not escape the harsh realities of tragedies, trials, and suffering people face, which they inevitably attribute mostly to their enemy, which may be the devil or humans who despise them or are jealous of their progress. In my culture, asking a woman her due date and rubbing her tummy when pregnant is inappropriate. I thought such beliefs probably were rooted in fear, so I did not strictly adhere to them after I crossed the three-month mark when pregnant with Isaac.

After losing him, I considered all angles in terms of the cause. I also reflected on the number of people that had rubbed my tummy, hopefully innocently, which I was unprepared for, which I thought nothing of then, and people whom I had told my due date. Since many people fell into this category, my mind began to consider if any, some, or all had something against me. Some were easily discarded from this list, and others I still wondered about. It got to a point where fear gripped me that I refused to discuss details about my pregnancy with my third baby, even with those close to me.

I remember one day the Lord saying to me, hey, they can't all be after you, and you will drive yourself nuts. He also pointed out that no evil could befall my baby or me because I was abiding under His shadow.

Believe

Although I lost Isaac and Faith and the enemy (devil) meant it for evil, I took many things out of the experience that I believe made the situation work together for my good, which I will highlight in the next section.

INSIGHTS GAINED

The following points are insights I gained as a result of my loss.

- Trials in our lives reveal how strong or weak our faith in God is.

- God does not want anything, even pain, to separate us from His love.

- As Christians, God wants us to remain strong in our faith, even in bad times.

- Conception and the ability to have children are blessings beyond a biological process, for which we should be thankful.

- Although my babies died, I need not grieve 'forever' as I have hope in God, they are in heaven, and we will be reunited.

- My experience is an opportunity to reach out to other women and families going through a similar situation.

Paradigm Shift

- It is a privilege to be entrusted with a baby(ies), but they are ultimately God's.
- Friends and family can be a great source of encouragement in grieving, but only God can truly comfort and give peace.
- I cannot receive from God if I subconsciously blame him for my misfortune.
- Although I experienced two significant catastrophes, I need not feel sorry for myself and wallow in self-pity as God has promised to replace my mourning with dancing.
- Despite my predicament, there are still loads for which to be grateful.
- I was created first to bring pleasure to God and not to be a mother only. I am complete because I am a child of God, and fulfillment will come from accomplishing the purpose for which He created me.

God wants us to remain strong in faith even in bad times.

Believe

WHERE ARE MY BABIES NOW?

When my babies died, I wanted to know what became of them. Where did they go? What do they look like? What will they be doing? Will we be reunited again? Will they recognize me when they see me in the future? What is heaven like? Some people believe that once babies die, they become angels and watch over their families on earth. To answer my questions, I found a useful book by John MacArthur, entitled *Safe in the Arms of God*. He goes into great detail about these issues. The answers I got for myself to these questions are as follows.

Both Isaac and Faith went instantly to heaven because they are below the age of accountability and cannot understand the issues of sin and salvation. Hence God considers them innocent and shows compassion. The Bible says that when Jesus Christ returns, those who are alive and are left on earth will be caught up together, with those who died in Christ, in the clouds to meet Jesus Christ in the air and be with Him forever. In other words, because I have accepted Jesus as my Lord and Savior, I, my husband, Isaac, Faith, and other children will be reunited forever in the future (1 Thessalonians 4:13-18). What comfort!

Paul in the Bible points out that heaven is definitely a better place than earth (Philippians 1:23) and even better than the imaginative world of Pandora in the sci-fi movie Avatar by James Cameron. It is a place where all tears are wiped away, no more death, crying, sorrow, and pain (Revelations 21:4). I remember the story of the rich man who died and went to heaven and saw Lazarus (Luke 16) who sat begging at his gate, he instantly recognized him. Likewise, I believe my children will recognize me and me likewise. Heaven has streets of Gold (Revelations 21:21). I believe it is more beautiful than anywhere on earth, including the seven wonders of the world.

1 Corinthians 15:49 points out that we humans, including babies, will bear the likeness of Jesus Christ. In heaven, God is praised and worshipped. Consequently, we will worship God all day and every day.

DO I STAND A CHANCE?

What do you do when you are in a dire situation?

How can you figure out what happened to you?

Where do you go when no one has answers for you?

Who do you turn to when the pain becomes unbearable?

How do you move forward when there are no guarantees?

Who can tell you what the future holds?

Believe

When should you try again?
Whose report should you believe?

This was my dilemma. These were the questions I wrestled with daily during this wilderness experience. I was afraid to try the third time. What if my baby died again? How was I so sure God won't let me down again? Perhaps I was not meant to be a mum. Thoughts like this ran through my mind. I had to fight it. I had been through so much as a woman (buried two children and not even thirty-five yet). Although I knew God was a good God, perhaps he allowed Isaac and Faith to die for a reason. So, what was his plan the third time round?

I had to read the scriptures from the Bible consciously — God's word to me in relation to having faith, becoming a mum, and God's miraculous power. It is so easy to forget what we read. Hence, I took it a step further by writing down these scriptures in a little 'purple' notebook and meditating on the words I read. My notebook went everywhere, so each time I felt discouraged and doubtful, I read and reread the word of God to build hope and a picture for my future as a mummy.

I also did loads of daydreaming. I thought about the day of delivery, what that moment would feel like when I held my son, how people would rejoice with me and congratulate me, the day my numerous visits to the hospital would end, pushing my son in his pram and going out with him and many other thoughts. The real thing is no way compared to my daydreams.

It is effortless to succumb to the tales of woe and medical prognosis we are given because that is all we can see at that point in time. To move myself from a place of anguish to anticipation, I had to begin to envisage what God could bring about in my life, irrespective of my past medical history and prognosis. I had to breathe, live, talk, stand on, and believe God's word. There were times I doubted if everything would turn out well, but when that happened, I went back to meditating on God's word until I believed it again.

Promises

Believe

7

FULL OF THE WORD & WONDERS

At the age of thirteen, I decided to ask Jesus to forgive my sins and guide me in everything I did. I made this commitment because I realized He created me, and the only way I could discover my purpose in life and live a fulfilled life was to be in an active relationship with him. Most people who believe in God most likely believe that there is another life after this; it is more than here and now. I believe in eternity and consciously came to acknowledge that this world is not my home after my son's death. The loss of my son helped me put things in the proper perspective and not put more of my efforts into gaining earthly recognition but heavenly recognition. Everything I do on earth will determine the feedback I will get in heaven when I see God.

Promises

I could only deal with my loss, believe in God that I would become a mum based on His promises, continue with my assignment on earth and look forward to eternity as a result of my Christian faith.

> *Everything I do on earth will determine the feedback I will get in heaven when I see God.*

This section is for you if you have not committed your life to Jesus Christ and invited Him into your heart as your Lord and Saviour. Or perhaps you have turned your back on your Christian faith because of the things life has thrown at you and the 'non-intervention' of God when you called on Him. God knows you, has a wonderful plan for you, and wants to have a vibrant and two-way relationship with you today!

Please say this prayer to ask Jesus into your life and to guide you as you enter into a relationship with Him:

Lord Jesus Christ,
I am sorry for the things I have done wrong in my life (ask His forgiveness for anything particular that is on your conscience). Please forgive me. I now turn from

everything I know is wrong. Thank you for dying on the cross for me so I can be forgiven and set free. Thank you for offering me forgiveness and the gift of the Holy Spirit. Please come into my life. Thank you, Lord Jesus.

WHAT NOW?

Tell friends and family about your decision.
Read the Bible.
Talk and fellowship with God daily.
Join and become committed in a lively church.

EXPERIENCING THE SUPERNATURAL

How did I see myself as a mummy again?

I reminded myself of God's love and dwelt on it.

I focused on His good plans for me based on His word.

I found out what God's opinion was regarding conception and childbirth.

I read real-life stories of women who were in a similar position both in bible times and present-day time.

I wrote down the list of all the baby things we needed and surfed the internet for the best deals. Even though I was not ready to buy these items but began to prepare.

Promises

I went to a Mother Care store and bought a pair of pink booties in anticipation of a third child. I wanted another girl because the time we spent with Faith was too short. This was an act of faith.

I spent time talking to my third baby and called him by name once we decided on a name.

I prayed for him regularly; growth in the womb, easy delivery, no abnormalities, and he won't be a stillbirth.

I understood that God is still in the business of miracles, so I can count on him.

My past did not need to determine my future.

Having a baby would be a source of encouragement to others.

I began to thank God because I saw it as a done deal.

I spoke to other mums and learned a few things about practical motherhood.

If God could allow a ninety-year-old woman (Sarah) to conceive and deliver safely without any medical intervention, I believed He could do mine many years after. I am always awed by God's wisdom and His creative ability. It's incredible how a baby is formed through a very intricate and complex process in a womb-like environment and thrives there for nine months. He can do the impossible regardless of how difficult your situation may seem. Read, Reflect, Recite and live the word. It works!

Believe

MY HOPE AFFIRMATIONS

Below are scriptures I found really encouraging and a source of strength while waiting for God's promise to be fulfilled in my life. I want to share with you how I strengthened my faith in God and believed in Him against the odds by meditating on His word. I lived on these scriptures and found them tremendously helpful while waiting expectantly for my third and fourth babies.

What I understood and took from each scripture is in bold beneath each Bible verse.

He can do the impossible regardless of how difficult your situation may seem.

Isaiah 41:10 (NIV Translation)
So do not fear, for I am with you; do not be dismayed,
For I am your God. I will strengthen you and help you;
I will uphold you with my righteous right hand.

God actually gave me this word when I was re-admitted to Hospital following Isaac's death with a raised blood pressure. This gave me hope all the way through to my second son's birth.

• • •

Isaiah 54:10 (NIV Translation)
Though the mountains be shaken and the hills be removed, Yet my unfailing love for you will not be shaken, Nor my covenant of peace be removed says the LORD, Who has compassion on you.

Irrespective of what had happened, I realized God indeed has compassion on me, and His peace with no anxiety was mine

• • •

Nahum 1:15 (The Message Translation)
Look! Striding across the mountains—a messenger bringing the latest good news: peace! a holiday, Judah! Celebrate! Worship and recommit to God! No more worries about this enemy.

Believe

This one is history. Close the books.

Stillbirth, preeclampsia, and high blood pressure would be history for me.

• • •

Romans 12:12 (King James Translation)
Rejoicing in hope; patient in tribulation; continuing instant in prayer.

My attitude while I am waiting should be of patience, prayer, and praise.

• • •

Exodus 23: 25–26 (New Living Translation)
You must serve only the Lord your God. If you do, I will bless you with food and water, and I will protect you from illness. There will be no miscarriages or infertility in your land, and I will give you long, full lives.

As I had served God even in my pain, my pregnancy would bring the expected outcome.

• • •

Exodus 1:19 (The Amplified Translation)
The midwives answered Pharaoh, "Because the Hebrew women are not like the Egyptian women; they are vigorous and give birth quickly and their babies are born before the midwife can get to them.

I believed God for a quick delivery and was actually surprised that only one midwife delivered my third baby; unlike Isaac and Faith, we had a room full of doctors and midwives.

• • •

Matthew 8:17 (New Living Translation)
This fulfilled the word of the Lord through the prophet Isaiah, who said, 'He took our sicknesses and removed our diseases.'

I thanked God that every trace of high blood pressure would be taken away.

• • •

1 John 4:18 (New Living Translation)
Such love has no fear, because perfect love expels all fear. If we are afraid, it is for fear of punishment, and this shows that we have not fully experienced his perfect love.

Believe

Since God loves me, there is no need for me to be afraid about the outcome of my pregnancy.

• • •

Philippians 4:13 (Amplified Translation)
I have strength for all things in Christ who empowers me. I am ready for anything and equal to anything through Him Who infuses inner strength into me; I am self-sufficient in Christ's sufficiency.

I need God's strength to go through all the stages of pregnancy, scans, and cervical stitch procedure.

• • •

Luke 1:37 (Amplified Translation)
For with God nothing is ever impossible and no word from God shall be without power or impossible of fulfillment.

God can do even the impossible, even intervene in the life of a woman with a poor obstetric history.

• • •

Promises

I John 5:14–15 (Amplified Translation)
And this is the confidence (the assurance, the privilege of boldness) which we have in Him: [we are sure] that if we ask anything (make any request) according to His will (in agreement with His own plan), He listens to and hears us.

God hears and answers so I can ask confidently.

• • •

Mark 11:23–24 (New Living Translation)
I tell you the truth, you can say to this mountain, 'May you be lifted up and thrown into the sea,' and it will happen. But you must really believe it will happen and have no doubt in your heart. I tell you, you can pray for anything, and if you believe that you've received it, it will be yours.

I really need to believe what I am asking God for.

• • •

Isaiah 54:13–15 (New Living Translation)
But in that coming day no weapon turned against you will succeed. You will silence every voice raised up to accuse you. These benefits are enjoyed by the servants of the Lord; their

Believe

vindication will come from me. I, the Lord, have spoken!

Whatever plans the enemy has won't happen.

• • •

Psalm 37:4 (Amplified Translation)
Delight yourself also in the Lord, and He will give you the desires and secret petitions of your heart.

Put God first, and He will honor my desires.

• • •

Hebrews 4:16 (New Living Translation)
So let us come boldly to the throne of our gracious God. There we will receive his mercy, and we will find grace to help us when we need it most.

When I hit rock bottom, I need to approach God.

• • •

1 Samuel 1:27 (NIV Translation)
I prayed for this child, and the LORD has granted me what I asked of him.

God answers prayers.

• • •

Promises

Genesis 20:22-23 (NIV Translation)
Then God remembered Rachel; he listened to her and opened her womb. She became pregnant and gave birth to a son and said, "God has taken away my disgrace."

Whatever I may have been tagged as or perceived, it can change.

• • •

Psalm 91:10 (King James Translation)
There shall no evil befall thee, neither shall any plague come nigh thy dwelling.

All the known or unknown infections in pregnancy won't be discovered in me.

• • •

Psalm 113: 9 (New Living Translation)
He gives the childless woman a family, making her a happy mother. Praise the Lord!

I will be a happy mum.

• • •

Psalm 128:3–4 (The Message Translation)
*Your wife will bear children as a vine bears grapes, your household lush as a vineyard,
the children around your table as fresh and promising as young olive shoots.
Stand in awe of God's Yes. Oh, how he blesses the one who fears God!*

I will have my own children.

• • •

Jeremiah 29:11 (Amplified Translation)
For I know the thoughts and plans that I have for you, says the Lord, thoughts and plans for welfare and peace and not for evil, to give you hope in your final outcome.

God surely has a good plan for me and my future so I can relax.

• • •

Psalm 34:4 (Amplified Translation)
I sought (inquired of) the Lord and required Him [of necessity and on the authority of His Word], and He heard me, and delivered me from all my fears.

I can be set free from my fears and do not need to live in terror.

• • •

2 Corinthians 10:5 (New Living Translation)
So humble yourselves before God. Resist the devil, and he will flee from you.

I need to stop accepting the victim tag and fight!

• • •

Ephesians 3:20 (The Message Translation)
God can do anything, you know—far more than you could ever imagine or guess or request in your wildest dreams!

Even if I can't comprehend it, He can do it.

• • •

Romans 8:37 (Amplified Translation)
Yet amid all these things we are more than conquerors and gain a surpassing victory through Him Who loved us.

Despite what has happened, I am still a conqueror.

• • •

Believe

2 Timothy 1:7 (Amplified Translation)
For God did not give us a spirit of timidity (of cowardice, of craven and cringing and fawning fear), but [He has given us a spirit] of power and of love and of calm and well-balanced mind and discipline and self-control.

Irrational thoughts will have no control over me; instead I will have a calm mind.

• • •

Psalm 112:7 (Amplified Translation)
He shall not be afraid of evil tidings; his heart is firmly fixed, trusting (leaning on and being confident) in the Lord.

I should not await bad news because I trust God.

• • •

Philippians 4: 6-7 (New Living Translation)
Don't worry about anything; instead, pray about everything. Tell God what you need, and thank him for all he has done. Then you will experience God's peace, which exceeds anything we can understand. His peace will guard your hearts and minds as you live in Christ Jesus.

Instead of worrying, I need to talk to God.

• • •

Promises

Psalm 32:8 (Amplified Translation)
I [the Lord] will instruct you and teach you in the way you should go; I will counsel you with my eye upon you.

Lord, I need guidance on what hospital to go to, what choices to make, and who to seek counsel from.

• • •

2 Corinthians 1:4 (New Living Translation)
He comforts us in all our troubles so that we can comfort others. When they are troubled, we will be able to give them the same comfort God has given us.

My pain is not in vain. It can inspire others.

• • •

Isaiah 66: 7-9 (The Message Translation)
Before she went into labor, she had the baby. Before the birth pangs hit, she delivered a son. Has anyone ever heard of such a thing? Has anyone seen anything like this? A country born in a day? A nation born in a flash? But Zion was barely in labor when she had her babies! Do I

open the womb and not deliver the baby? Do I, the One who delivers babies, shut the womb?

God can do things instantly, and He won't bring me to the end and then abandon me.

• • •

Isaiah 65:23 (The Message Translation)
No more sounds of weeping in the city, no cries of anguish; no more babies dying in the cradle.

A friend of ours shared this scripture with us. No more will I have another dead baby.

• • •

Galatians 3:13-14 (The Message Translation)
Christ redeemed us from that self-defeating, cursed life by absorbing it completely into himself. Do you remember the Scripture that says, "Cursed is everyone who hangs on a tree"? That is what happened when Jesus was nailed to the cross: He became a curse, and at the same time dissolved the curse. And now, because of that, the air is cleared, and we can see that Abraham's blessing is present and available for non-Jews, too. We are all able to receive God's life, his Spirit, in and with us by believing—just the way Abraham received it.

Promises

I do not need to pay for my sins or that of my parents. It's been paid for once I accepted Jesus Christ as my Lord.

• • •

Psalm 138:8 (New King James Translation)
The LORD will perfect that which concerns me; your mercy, O LORD, endures forever; do not forsake the works of your hands.

My story will have a beautiful ending.

Believe

Only If
© Funke Oham

Only if I had done things differently
Decided carefully on the choices before me
Perhaps my story would have been different

Only if I had paid closer attention
Refused to take things by face value
Perhaps my story would have been different

Only if I had kept to time
Realized the effect of missing my appointment
Perhaps my story would have been different

Only if our paths never crossed
Subjected to the pain your oversight caused me
Perhaps my story would have been different

Only if I had been more discerning
Pondered and prayed more about my dreams
Perhaps my story would have been different

Only If

Only if I can just be still
Only if I can just stop the blame game
Only if I can just recognize what happened to me
Only if I can just see the good in the bad

Only if I can just let my ache be my past
Only if I can just praise in my pain
Only if I can just see tomorrow in my today
Only if I can just trust in spite of my 'whys'

Then I will be free again
Then I will be able to carry on
Then I will be an inspiration to others
Then I will be courageous to try again

Then I will be admired and not pitied
Then I will be a blessing and not a burden
Then I will be all I was made to be
Then I will start a brand-new day

Believe

ABOUT THE AUTHOR

Funke is an award-winning mentor, author and speaker. Her first book 'Always a Mum: How I survived my baby loss' addresses issues of motherhood in relation to loss, living again and finding purpose in pain. In July 2021, Funke launched The Waiting Room — an online support community for women (open to men) who are trying to conceive and have experienced baby loss. She brings her vibrant messages to women's conferences, leadership forums and career events.

Find out more at
www.funkeoham.com

About the Author

Printed in Great Britain
by Amazon